Dedicated to Mother Superior E
for suggesting my talents wei
priesthood.

Scamtoons by Cal
Dice & Card Illustrations by Tony Dunn
Cover Design by Liz Kaufman
Edited by Matthew Field

Second Edition 2018

About the author
Mister Big 'N' Fast Bobby Knuckles is the pseudonym for a Vatican exorcist. If possessed, contact DEVIL_GOT_ME.COM

Beat'em, Cheat'em, Leave'em Bleedin' Copyright ™ & © 1994, 2018, Every Trick In The Book Inc. All rights reserved. No part of this book may be reproduced in any form or by any electronic or mechanical means, including information storage and retrieval systems, without permission in writing from the publisher, except by a reviewer, who may quote brief passages in a review. Published by Every Trick In The Book Inc., Box 1262, Brockville, Ontario, Canada K6V 5W2. Printed in the U.S.A. by Houdini Magic under exclusive license from Every Trick In The Book Inc.

CONTENTS

INTRODUCTION 1

WHERE TO GET MARKED CARDS LOADED DICE AND DOUBLE-HEADED COINS 3

DOUBLE-HEADED COINS 5
    CON OF THE REALM 5
    POCKET CHANGE 6
    TWO HEADS ARE BETTER THAN ONE 6
    TWO OUT OF THREE AIN'T BAD 6
    NONE OUT OF THREE 8
    TWO OUT OF THREE AIN'T BADDER 8
    HEADS I WIN, TAILS YOU LOSE 9
    A PENNEY FOR YOUR THOUGHTS 9

MARKED CARDS 13
    TEN CARDS, TWENTY FINGERS, UNLIMITED CASH 13
    THE GAME OF 31 15
    AC/DC DEAL 17

MONTES & POKER SCAMS 19
    SVENGALI MONTE 19
    TWO-CARD MONTE 21
    THREE-CARD MONTE 22
    JIGGERY POKERY 23

LOADED DICE 25
    ANOTHER GAME OF 31 25
    BONE DRY 26
    PAIR OF DICE BY THE DASHBOARD LIGHT 28
    A SIMPLE DICE SWITCH 28
    BET NOIRE 28
    MONTE BONES 29
    OTHER IDEAS 37
    GAME OF BONES 37
    OIL & WATER DICE 39
    5-3-4-1-6-2 41
    COUNT DICEULA 44

THE CHICAGO BAR SCAM 45
    CHICAGO BAR CARD SCAM 46

CHEATING: SACRED HERITAGE & YOUR NEW HOBBY

"Do they have to be honest?"
—W.C. Fields
(when asked if he would like to make a few honest dollars for himself.)

"The first duty of a revolutionary is to get away with it."
—Abbie Hoffman

INTRODUCTION

THE UNIVERSAL LOOPHOLE: Hard work and easy money never find themselves together. It is even an article of faith with some that the more effortless the cash collection, the more probable the hand of the devil.

An honest living throws up so many moral, ethical, religious and legal constraints that modern men and women may never venture to cheat, scam, hoodwink and clip their friends and thus they may never feel the decadent thrill that comes *only* from doing just that.

HERE IT IS: But I've got good news, real good news, a loophole so big you can scam all day and still go home at night feeling that if this was another time and place, your eligibility to carry the Ten Commandments down from the mountain and start a new religion would be completely unaffected.

WORD UP BRO'—'CAUSE—

If you want to steal from the suckers, simply tell them so.

That's right.

- Tell them that you will be taking their money.
- Tell them that they have no chance of winning.
- Tell them that no matter how fair or how impossible your proposal is, they will still lose, all the time, every time, for all time because—
- You *will be* cheating them.

Why then would anyone venture to bet a penny?

MY FAVORITE DEADLY SIN: Greed, naturally.

That's because not only do you tell the marks that they will lose their money, you *also* tell them that they may learn something, something that may make *them* a lot of money.

Yes—that's right my man, they may learn just how the scam going down works. And if they do, then that day, and the next day and every day from then on, they can go out in the world and use that knowledge to make money. Big money, friendly money, easy money. They will never pay for a drink again as long as they live.

THIS AIN'T NO GAMBLIN', THIS AIN'T NO FOOLIN' AROUND: So they're not *betting* with you, they're paying tuition, because this is less a con game than a lesson in conning, less a risk than an investment, not a sin but a virtue, a virtual act of empowerment. Praise the Lord and pass the suckers.

And in the result, you are being totally honest about your dishonesty and if the marks want to continue, the sin is theirs, not yours. The downtime in Hell has been transferred from your soul to the soul of the sucker. If only programming your VCR was this simple.

LOVE: Now this approach has a number of positive results, in addition to the star on the afterlife report card. First, set up this way, marks almost never balk at handing over the cash (how could they, since by playing they've agreed it's okay for you to take it). Second, people love this kind of thing, even when they lose. In every soul, no matter how pure, there is always a dark corner that resonates near larceny, thrills in the presence of swindle, sings when the hustle is imminent.

CHARITY: But why should I tell you about all this? What are my motives? Well, as a condition of my parole and to fulfill the community service obligation, I am forced to share with you the best parts of my large collection of bar betchas, scams, cons and skewed proposals and propositions so that you may never fall victim to them, Whether your victim falls is up to you, because—

HOPE: —I would never suggest that anyone should use this information to cheat those not fortunate enough to have purchased this little volume. Rather, if used, I would hope the objective would only be to entertain, stimulate the intellect or bring a little light to those huddled in the darkness of ignorance. Good luck—but you won't need it. You will need some other stuff, though, so turn the page and get your wallet out.

WHERE TO GET MARKED CARDS LOADED DICE AND DOUBLE-HEADED COINS

"The prince should never attempt to win by force what he might otherwise win by fraud."
—Machiavelli, The Prince

TOOLS OF THE TRADE: Yes, you're going to need a few things to start down the crooked road to financial independence, things you won't find in MallWart, things not spoken of in polite company, things you've heard about but probably have never seen. Stuff that could get you stoned to death in certain third world fundamentalist countries and parts of Tennessee, but stuff that, thanks to democracy, the fifth amendment and the capitalist system is easily found here in America.

CHEATS 'R' US: It hasn't been invented yet, but you and the other scamsters looking to load up on marked cards, loaded dice, double-headed coins and the other baggage of this twisted trade, can find all you need easily—*do a Google search.*

Try Googling, "marked cards," "loaded dice," "double-headed coins" and "magicians' supplies." Check phone listings: in any large city for magic shops: magicians and con men use the same techniques (e.g. lying) and sometimes the same equipment, though for different purposes (magicians create the illusion of the impossible, con men, the illusion of the square deal).

CHARGE IT: Place your order using your or someone else's credit card number and the nasty bits will be delivered to your door almost immediately. You can be recovering your investment from your eager victims within a few days.

SWINDLE TECH: Remember this tricky stuff is the tools of your trade, not just mere novelties. Their purchase is an investment in your financial future. Keeping their existence secret is an investment in staying alive and maintaining fully-functioning arms, legs and fingers. Today you're scamming beer money, tomorrow you're doing six to ten for real estate fraud. It's a golden road, so get on it as soon as possible.

Here's your shopping list:

Double-Tailed Quarter

Double-Headed Quarter

Marked Cards

Stripper Deck

DeLand Dollar Deck

Svengali Deck

Ordinary Decks To Match

Three Card Monte

Sucker Card Trick

Two Card monte

7–11 dice

Poker Dice

YOUR FRIENDLY NEIGHBORHOOD MAGIC DEALER
HAS WHAT YOU NEED

DOUBLE-HEADED COINS

> "God was left out of the Constitution but was furnished a front seat on the coins of the country."
> —Mark Twain, *Mark Twain In Eruption*

THE POWER: The proper use of double-headed and double-tailed coins is known to few. As a result, even though the existence of such coins is well known, they can be used most effectively to suck the cash right out your Mark's tight little fist. Keep in mind that in all these bets, you're always flipping for something worth much more than the coins used (a free drink, fifty bucks, a Porsche, ownership of a savings and loan in California, etc.)—the coins are simply the game pieces, not the prize.

CON OF THE REALM

THE BET: You offer to flip a coin for fifty bucks. The Mark gets to call it while the coin is in the air (this, of course, would prevent any control of the coin being effective).

THE OUTCOME: You always win.

THE SCAM: A double-headed coin is used. If the Mark calls, "heads," you grab the coin out of the air, and say, "No bet—I just wanted to see if you were a gambling man." If the Mark calls, "tails," you let the coin fall to the ground.

The psychology here is most devious: when the Mark loses he can never suspect a double-headed coin since he got to call while the coin was in the air (and a double-sided coin in those circumstances is useless).

POCKET CHANGE

THE BET: The Mark flips a coin. You flip a second coin. If you match the mark's flip, you win.

THE OUTCOME: You win every time.

THE SCAM: You'll need a double-headed quarter and a double-tailed quarter. Have these in your pocket with some dimes, nickels and pennies (but no other quarters). After the mark flips his coin, reach in your pocket and remove the handful of change. You can easily remove the gaffed quarter you need to win. Flip it and collect your winnings.

Or, you can remove the wrong coin and intentionally lose. After you do, return the coin to the change in your hand and suggest a rematch for double or nothing. This time you ensure a win.

PUTTING THE MUSCLE IN YOUR HUSTLE
In any scam where you control the outcome, play three times, losing the first two times. Then bet big and win the third round.

TWO HEADS ARE BETTER THAN ONE

THE BET: You and two other guys flip coins. The odd man out wins.

THE OUTCOME: You and your secret partner win whenever you want.

THE SCAM: You'll need a double-tailed and a double-headed coin and a covert confederate. Your friend is in on the scam, but the mark doesn't know it. You have the double-headed coin in your pocket change and your pal has the double-tailed coin in his. You can start to play the game legit, with regular coins from your pocket change, but when it comes time to drain the Mark of all his cash, you flip your double-head coin and your team-mate flips his double-tailed coin.

The odd man out wins—but this has to be either you or your associate since the Mark's flip (heads or tails) has to match either your coin (heads) or your accomplice's (tails).

TWO OUT OF THREE AIN'T BAD

THE BET: The Mark begins to shake three quarters together in his fist. Asked to pick heads or tails, he picks heads. The coins are thrown to the table. If two or more heads show up, the Mark wins; if two or more tails show up, you win.

THE OUTCOME: The Hustler wins 75% of the time.

THE SCAMS: There are actually three scams running here: a double-tailed coin, lying about the odds and making up the rules as you go along. You'll need a double-tailed quarter and two ordinary quarters to match.

FORCING TAILS: Hand the three coins to the Mark and have him start shaking them in his fist. If you do this casually, selecting the coins from your pocket change (making sure you include the gaffed coin), the Mark will suspect nothing. Now you ask him a very sneaky question:

"What shall we use, heads or tails?"

If he replies, "Tails," you say:

"Tails. Okay, throw the coins down and if two or more tails come up, you pay me ten bucks, but if two or more heads come up, I'll pay you ten bucks."

If he replies, "Heads," you say, "Heads. Okay, throw the coins down and if two or more heads come up, I'll pay you ten bucks, but if two or more tails come up, you'll pay me ten bucks."

You always word it so that he pays you ten bucks if two or more tails come up.

THE ODDS: This is a percentage bet: that means that over time you'll win more than you lose, but you will lose 25% of the time. However, your losses are further reduced because you are betting even money, your dollar against the Mark's dollar, when you should be betting three dollars against the Mark's single dollar. Here's why: if you were tossing out three regular quarters, there are only eight ways they can land:

H H H	H T T
H H T	T H T
H T H	T T H
T H H	T T T

Since two or more tails occur half the time (see the bold outcomes above), this is an even chance bet: to be fair, you and your opponent would each risk an equal amount of money, you betting on two or more tails, he betting against it. But when one of the coins is double-tailed, there aren't eight possibilities, there are only four and two tails come up 75% of the time:

T H H
T H T
T T H
T T T

Since two or more tails come up three out of four times (see the bold outcomes above), a fair bet would your three dollars against your opponent's one dollar. However, with this scam you bet even money, which means the Mark is risking more money than he should and you are risking less.

And of course there is the fine psychological misdirection of the Mark seeing combinations of heads and tails. The use of a double coin seems impossible. This principle is also used in the next scam.

NONE OUT OF THREE

THE BET: You and the Mark each throw five bucks into the pot. The Mark begins to shake three quarters together in his fist. Asked to pick heads or tails, he picks heads. The coins are thrown to the table.

If three heads show up, the Mark wins; if three tails show up, you win. If there is a mix of heads and tails, nobody wins, and each party throws five more bucks into the pot.

Now it's your turn. You shake the coins and throw them down. If three heads show up, the Mark wins; if three tails show up, you win. If there is a mix of heads and tails, nobody wins and each party again throws five bucks into the pot.

This back and forth continues until somebody wins.

THE OUTCOME: You win 100% of the time.

THE SCAMS: One of the coins is double-tailed and you once again make up the rules depending on what the spectator chooses.

As he shakes the three coins in his fist, you ask:

"What shall we use, heads or tails?"

If he replies, "Tails," you say:

"Tails. Okay, throw the coins down and if three tails come up, I win the pot, but if three heads come up, you win."

If he replies, "Heads," you say, "Heads. Okay, throw the coins down and if three heads come up, you win the pot, but if three tails come up, I win."

You always word it so that you win the pot if three tails come up.

THE ODDS: If one of the coins is double-tailed, there are only four possibilities:

```
T H H
T H T
T T H
T T T
```

Three heads are impossible; the *only* winning combination is three tails (see the bold outcome above). What makes this good is that there are three combinations where nobody wins and these will occur 75% of the time allowing for a nice fat pot by the time your winner comes up.

TWO OUT OF THREE AIN'T BADDER

THE BET: The Mark shakes three quarters together in his fist and then throws them down on the table. You explain there are only three ways the coins can fall: all heads, all tails or some combination of heads and tails. If the coins come up all heads or all tails, the spectator wins, otherwise you win. So he has a two to one advantage and to be even fairer you offer to bet even money. Now the spectator shakes the coins again and throws them out.

THE OUTCOME: You win 75% of the time.

THE SCAM: No double coin is used here, just three ordinary quarters. The scam here is in misstating the odds. I'm including this swindle here, because after you've cleaned the guy out with *your* quarters, you might suggest his luck would improve if he used his own coins. This allows you to ditch the gaffed coins and finish in a state of grace.

THE ODDS: Your description of the odds sounds convincing: there are only three combinations possible, all heads, all tails or some combination of heads and tails. In fact there are eight combinations and six of those (see the bold outcomes below) are winners for you:

         H H H   **H T T**
        H H T **T H T**
        H T H **T T H**
        T H H T T T

The true odds here are exactly the same as the ones in "Two Out Three Ain't Bad," but here the gaff is in the lie, while there the gaff was in the coin.

HEADS I WIN, TAILS YOU LOSE

THE BET: The Mark picks tails. A handful of quarters—8 or 9—are mixed and dropped on the table. All the tails are eliminated and the coins mixed and thrown again. This is repeated until one of two things happen: there is one coin left—a head—in which case the Mark loses; or, there are no coins left, in which case the Mark wins.

THE OUTCOME: You always win.

THE SCAM: A double-headed quarter is used. To force the Mark into losing, ask him, "Heads or tails?" and then interpret his answer so that tails will be eliminated. If he says, "Tails," say, "Okay, we'll eliminate the tails on every throw." If he says, "Heads," say, "Heads—if there's a head left, you lose." After that, just follow the game along and you will win.

A PENNEY FOR YOUR THOUGHTS

In one of those diabolic coincidences that in darker and more ignorant times might be interpreted as evidence for the existence of a supreme being, a mathematician named Walter Penney discovered a marvelous mathematical fact: when tossing coins heads or tails, a situation can be created that will turn the odds in your favor, even with straight coins.

THE GAME

As described by Karl Fulves (*Epilogue*, No. Ten, November 1970, p.77), a game using Penney's discovery can be played with three coins.

The three coins will each be individually flipped and placed one after the other in a row on the table.

Before the first combination is produced, the two players each guess which three-way combination will come up first. For example, the Mark picks HHH; the Hustler THH.

The coins are each flipped and laid out. Assume THT is the result as shown below.

That combination doesn't match either guess, so the coin at the left end of the row is flipped and placed at the right end of the row. Assume the new combination is HTH. Still no winner.

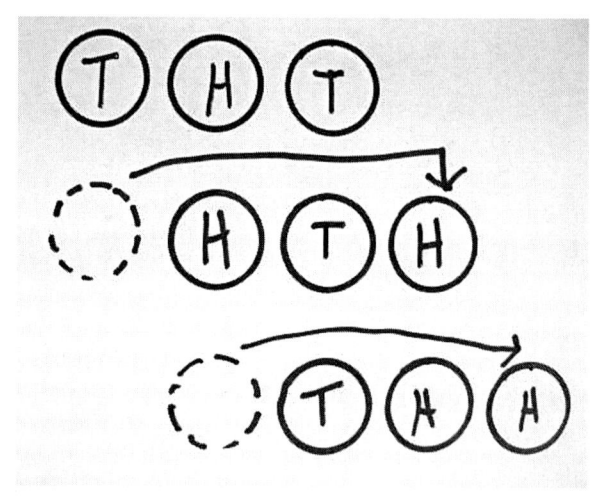

THE SCAM

This appears to be a perfectly even game, the odds 50/50 and in no one's favor. In fact, shockingly and against all intuition and experience, the odds in the Hustler's favor range from two to one to seven to one.

Though there are only eight combinations that can occur:

HHH TTT HHT TTH HTT THH HTH THT

Each *successive* combination is *dependent* upon the prior combination.

For example, assume the first combination is THT and the second is HTH.

The second combination is made up of two coins from the first combination (i.e., HT)—and this second combination can *only be* either HTH or HTT.

Penney discovered that because each sequence is *dependent* on the one before it (unlike usual coin flipping where each flip is independent), the odds are never 50/50.

For example, if the Mark picks TTT and the Hustler picks HTT, the odds are 7 to 1 in the Hustler's favor that HTT will appear *before* TTT.

This, like Rock, Paper Scissors, is a non-transitive game: no matter what choice the Mark makes, the Hustler can choose a combination likely to beat him (in a transitive game, like Poker, there is a hierarchy of values and the higher value always wins).

The consolidated odds for each choice by the Mark and the Hustler are as follows:

MARK	HUSTLER	ODDS
TTT	HTT	7 to 1
HHH	THH	7 to 1
TTH	HTT	3 to 1
HHT	THH	3 to 1
THH	TTH	2 to 1
HTT	HHT	2 to 1

- 11 -

THT	TTH	2 to 1
HTH	HHT	2 to 1

The Edge

To ensure you always have the biggest advantage, you do two things.

First, always bet even money. The odds are always in your favor, but there's no point in advertising that fact by betting asymmetrically. You want the Mark to think that you both have the same chance of winning, that the game is a 50/50 proposition.

Second, you must always make the Mark pick his triplet first. Once he does, you choose your triplet by taking his and mentally modifying it in accordance with some simple rules.

Rule 1

Drop the last symbol on the right. He says TTH. You mentally convert that to the pair TT by dropping the H.

Rule 2

Look at the symbol on the right end of the pair. Add that to the left end of the pair. The symbol on the right end of TT is T which when added to the left end of the pair gives the triplet TTT.

Rule 3

Change the first symbol of the new triplet to its opposite. So TTT becomes HTT. This is the triplet you announce as yours.

Simple Formula

There is another way to formulate the odds-on combination.

Your first symbol is always the opposite of the Mark's second symbol. So if the Mark's triplet is TTH, your triplet starts with an H.

Your second and third symbols are the same as his first and second symbols. So you add TT to your H to get HTT.

HOW THE MARK SEES HIMSELF

HOW YOU SEE THE MARK

MARKED CARDS

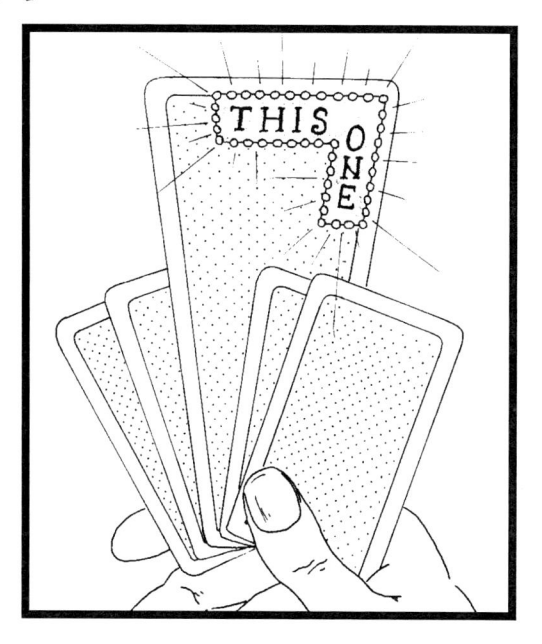

"Mundus vult decipi decipiatur ergo."
(The world wants to be cheated, so cheat.)
—Xaviera Hollander, The Happy Hooker

RENAISSANCE MAN: Around 1520, the aptly named Gerolamo Cardano, scholar, teacher and gambler, was the first to describe the use of marked cards in his Liber de Ludo Aleae (Book On Games of Chance).

During the writing of this chapter, I spontaneously began to speak and understand 16th century Italian, took to dressing strangely and pirouetting grotesquely in public and I now believe that my soul was briefly inhabited by Cardano, my spiritual predecessor.

Cards are marked in different ways and the deck you buy will come with full instructions for reading the backs. Usually, the marks are in the upper left corners. This chapter won't deal with the use of marked cards in standard card games, since the advantage there should be obvious. Rather, I'll concentrate on some fast scams and short cons that use a combination of marked cards and other methods to quickly and easily enhance your fiscal momentum at the expense of all those who innocently inquire, "Wanna play cards?"

TEN CARDS, TWENTY FINGERS, UNLIMITED CASH

THE BET: You and the Mark take turns shuffling ten cards and dealing out two five-card poker hands.

THE OUTCOME: You take home the cash.

THE SCAM: When the uninitiated think of using marked cards they usually assume that you have to read all the cards to figure out what to do. But this isn't necessarily so and anyway it's way too much work for the dilettante scamster. That's why this scam is so chillin': you only have to keep track of one card, the Card O' Doom.

As you'll see, whenever the Mark gets the Card O' Doom, he will lose and that's all you have to know to bet accordingly. I'm assuming you know the standard rules of poker and what hand beats what hand. If you don't, you'll be toast if you try this.

THE SET-UP: From your deck of marked cards remove three fives, three queens, three aces and one king. The king is the Card O' Doom. Try this experiment: shuffle the ten cards and deal out two hands face up. You'll see that the losing hand is the one with the Card O' Doom, the king. No matter how many times you shuffle and deal, the losing hand will always contain the Card O' Doom. In fact, there are only three possible combinations of hands:

full house beating three of a kind

three of a kind beating two pairs

two pairs beating one pair

And remember—the king will always be in the losing hand.

THE COME-ON: As you remove the cards from the deck, tell the Mark that the fairest form of poker is *Blind Ten Card No Draw*. Only ten cards are used and they are continually shuffled and dealt, so there's a fair chance that if you didn't get the cards the first time, you'll get them the second. And of course, by limiting the number of cards, cheating is impossible.

And there's one other feature: the cards are dealt face down and the betting is done before the cards are seen by the players.

In a variation, the players turn their cards face up one by one, betting more as each card is revealed.

THE GAME: Take turns shuffling and dealing two hands. Since the king is marked, you will immediately know who has the winning hand (that is, whomever gets the king loses) and you can bet accordingly. Remember the cards are face down and the betting occurs before they are turned face up.

By betting with the cards face down, it appears that the game is simply a game of chance with no advantage to either player.

ALMOST REAL POKER: To make the game appear more like real poker, have several rounds of betting like this: Have two hands dealt by dealing 5 cards in a row to each player (if the cards are dealt in a row you can easily spot the marked king).

Each player turns one card face up and either bets or folds. Continue to do this until all cards are face up and the winner known.

Of course, you know who the winner will be before a single card is turned over, so you can adjust your betting and folding appropriately.

STRIP SEARCH: Magic shops also sell *Stripper* decks. These are decks where the cards have been shaved (or stripped) so that one end is wider than the other. If a card is removed from this deck and turned end for end and reinserted, it can easily be found—even if the deck is shuffled—because the edges stick out.

Magic dealers sell a *marked* stripper deck called a *DeLand Dollar Deck*. If you use this deck for this hustle, you could set up the ten cards so their sides protrude. Now the Mark can shuffle the deck and you can still strip-out the ten cards you need and proceed (how to strip out the cards is described in the instructions that come with the deck).

THE GAME OF 31

THE GAME: Six cards, the ace, 2, 3, 4, 5 and 6 of spades, are mixed around face down on the table. You and the Mark alternately turn cards face-up and count to 31 using the values revealed.

The first person to reach 31 wins. If any one goes over 31, they lose.

THE OUTCOME: You can win or lose, as you like.

THE SCAM: In addition to the marked cards, you use a simple system that makes you a winner whenever you want.

THE RULES OF THE GAME: There is a bit more to the game than just described, but not much more. First, I'll describe the basic game, then I'll describe the secret system that lets you win.

Lay the six cards (A-2-3-4-5-6) face up on the table (when you can play and understand the game with the cards face-up, it is just as easy to do it with the cards face down, but I'll save the fine points on that for later).

Incidentally, the ace counts as 1.

PLAY: The Mark touches any card and calls out its value. For example, he might pick the 6 and say, "Six."

You now get to choose any card the Mark *didn't pick*. He picked a 6 so you can choose any one of the ace, 2, 3, 4 or 5.

You touch one of the cards, add its value to the Mark's and call out the total. For example, you might pick the 4, and say, "Ten" (the Mark chose 6, you chose 4—and 6+4=10).

Now the Mark responds. He can pick the 6 again, or the ace, 2, 3 or 5, but he can't pick the 4 because you just used it. Assume he picks the 2; the new total is 12 (6+4+2=12).

Now you go again, following the same rule: you can pick any card as long as it isn't the one the Mark just used. This goes on until a player reaches a total of 31 (this is a win) or a player goes over 31 (this is a loss).

SAMPLE GAME: A game might go like this, with you winning:

Round	Player	Chosen Number	total
1	Mark	6	6
2	You	4	10
3	Mark	2	12
4	You	5	17
5	Mark	6	23
6	You	ace	24
7	Mark	6	30
8	You	ace	31

THE DIRTY SECRET: As long as you make certain magic numbers as the game proceeds you can't lose. As the total changes with each move by the Mark, you always pick a number that will bring you up to the next magic number. The magic numbers are:

$$3 \quad 10 \quad 17 \quad 24$$

Note that each number is exactly 7 numbers higher than the previous number:

$$3 \quad +7 \quad 10 \quad +7 \quad 17 \quad +7 \quad 24$$

This makes memorizing the progression simple if you can remember the first number in the series, 3 (and that should be easy since the game is called "31"). Consider the sample game again. I've bolded the magic numbers so you can see how I made choices to ensure a win.

Round	Player	Chosen Number	Total
1	Mark	6	6
2	You	4	**10**
3	Mark	2	12
4	You	5	**17**
5	Mark	6	23
6	You	ace	**24**
7	Mark	6	30
8	You	ace	31

Here is another sample game with the magic numbers bolded. Note that you sometimes don't hit all the numbers, but you have plenty of chances to get as many as possible.

Round	Player	Chosen Number	Total
1	Mark	2	2
2	You	6	8
3	Mark	3	11

4	You	6	**17**
5	Mark	5	22
6	You	2	**24**
7	Mark	6	30
8	You	ace	31

PLAYING FACE-DOWN: Since the cards are marked, you can play this game face down with ease. You and the Mark simply turn the cards face-up to announce the value and the new total and then turn the cards face down again. This seems to add an additional complication to the game and seems to give an advantage to the player who can remember what card is where. Of course, it doesn't, but you claim that it does. Each game is played by shuffling the cards and dealing them face down haphazardly on the table so that in each game the cards are in different positions.

SURE-FIRE WINNERS AND LOSERS: It doesn't matter who goes first, but if you start with an ace, 2 or 5, winning is easy. Start with a 3, 4 or 6 for an easy loss.

AC/DC DEAL

THE GAME: The Mark shuffles the deck and deals out ten cards in a face-up row. You and the Mark take turns removing cards from either end of the row. The cards in each hand are added up (Aces = 1, court cards = 10) and the person with the highest total wins.

THE OUTCOME: You can win or lose, as you like.

THE SCAM: You can always predict the winning total and you can control how the cards are taken.

An example will show how this works. Assume the Mark has dealt out ten cards as follows:

| 4H | 3D | 2H | 2C | 6S | 7H | KC | 10S | QH | 3S |

Starting at the left end of the row with the 4H, total every second card:

| **4H** | 3D | **2H** | 2C | **6S** | 7H | **KC** | 10S | **QH** | 3S |

$$4+2+6+10+10 = 32$$

Starting at the left end of the row with the 3D, total every second card thereafter:

| 4H | **3D** | 2H | **2C** | 6S | **7H** | KC | **10S** | QH | **3S** |

$$3+2+7+10+3 = 25$$

There is only one game rule: cards can only be taken from either end of the row. Cards cannot be taken from the middle of the row.

To win with the cards in this example, you go first and take the 4H from the left end of the row, leaving the row like this:

— 18 —

| 3D | 2H | 2C | 6S | 7H | KC | 10S | QH | 3S |

The Mark now has two choices: he can take the 3D from the left end of the row or the 3S from the right end of the row. Assuming he takes the 3D, the row now looks like this for your choice:

| 2H | 2C | 6S | 7H | KC | 10S | QH | 3S |

You can take the 2H or the 3S. How do you decide? You use the secret scam rule: you take the card that was next to the card the Mark took. In this example, you'd take the 2H. In doing so, don't make it obvious: take a few beats to apparently "consider" your options. Mathematician Colm Mulcahy calls the principle on which this scam is based the Position Parity Principle and defines it this way:

> Take turns selecting cards, always choosing from one of the two exposed ends, then if you go first and start by taking the first card in the row, you'll end up with all of the cards in the odd positions. If you start by taking the last card in the row, you'll get the cards in the even positions.
>
> —"Position Parity," pp. 71-73, *Mathematical Card Magic* by Colm Mulcahy

After the Mark deals out the ten cards, you secretly total the odd cards and the even cards to determine which group is the winner and then proceed from there. You need some time to do this as well as a rationale so as you study the cards say you're memorizing all the combinations.

Explain the rules:

> "We'll take turns taking cards from either end of the row. You can't take a card from inside the row. When we both have five cards, we'll add the cards up—Aces equal one, court cards equal ten—and whoever has the higher total, wins.
>
> If it's a draw—same totals—we both add more money to the pot and ten more cards are dealt out."

A draw, though possibly rare, is good for you, since on the next round you'll win more money.

The best response when questioned by the vice squad.

MONTES & POKER SCAMS

"If you can't spot the sucker in the game in the first 10 minutes, then it must be you."
—Poker saying.

SVENGALI MONTE

THE BET: The Mark tries to find the ace of spades.

THE OUTCOME: He fails every time.

THE SCAM: A marvelous trick deck.

THE SCAMARIO: The Three-Card Monte normally seen on the streets of New York requires a skillful handling of the cards and years of practice normally acquired doing time in a large penal institution.

Luckily, the little hustle about to be described requires no skill, so if you are doing time in a large penal institution, you will still have plenty of spare hours to whittle that gun out of a bar of soap, draft your appeal and hope the governor calls before they throw the switch on the chair.

There is a bit more to the betting than described above, so stay tuned and listen up, here's the way the bets really go, followed by the sinister secret.

THE FIRST BET: After the deck has been cut into three piles and the Mark has chosen one of the top cards of a pile (e.g. the ace of spades), you offer to pay him $50 if he can find that card two out of three times as you shift the piles around on the table. If he loses he pays you $5. But he gets the wrong card on the first try, so—

THE SECOND BET: —you make it easier by saying you'll give him $50 if he finds the ace on the second or third try. But he again he gets the wrong card, so—

THE THIRD BET: —you say you'll make it even easier for him. Since he's much better at finding the wrong card (he's done that twice already), if he gets a wrong card on the third try, he wins the $50.

But if he gets an ace, he loses and has to finally pay you the $5.

And to make it even easier for him, you'll use just three cards and move very, very slowly.

The Mark places his finger on his chosen card. You remove the other cards. He turns his card over and weeps—it's the ace and he loses the third and final time!

THE SET-UP: You'll need a trick deck sold in magic shops as the *Svengali* deck. Even though this appears to be an ordinary deck, the cards can be shown to be all different or all the same. One second the deck can look ordinary—a mixture of different cards—and the next moment it can be shown to be all the same card (e.g. all aces of spades).

Of course, if you value your life, you're never going to show anyone that the deck can undergo such a miraculous morphing. Besides, before this little scam is over the trick deck will be switched for an ordinary one, just in case some curious soul wants to check the cards.

THE SVENGALI PRINCIPLE: The deck is made up of 26 different cards and 26 duplicate force cards (say 26 ace of spades ("AS")).

The 26 duplicates are cut short and then paired with the 26 assorted cards. If the deck is riffled from face to back, all different cards are seen.

Riffled in the opposite direction, every card is the same.

If you hold the deck by its ends and cut it, you will always cut to one of the force cards (one of the short cards).

Full instructions come with such decks, and if you play with one for an evening, you'll have all the familiarity you'll need.

You also need an ordinary deck to match the *Svengali* (same color, same back design). Remove the card from this deck that matches the force card in the *Svengali*. So if the force card in the *Svengali* is the ace of spades, remove the ace of spades from your ordinary deck and discard it.

Take the ordinary deck out of its case and place it in your right coat pocket. Cut a force card to the top of the *Svengali* deck, place the deck in its case and put it in the same pocket as the ordinary deck.

When ready for the big pay-off, take the *Svengali* out and remove it from its case. Put the case in your right pocket with the duplicate deck. Casually show all the cards to be different (you do this by riffling from the face as explained in the instructions that come with the deck). Now do this:

THREE PILES: Cut the deck into three more or less equal piles by holding the deck on the ends. This will cut an AS to the top of each pile (that is, there will be a short force card on top of each pile).

The Mark points to any pile. You turn over the top card of that pile showing the force card, the AS, and you drop this card, *still face up*, on top of one of the *other* piles. Now turn over the next card in the chosen pile—this will be another value—and using it as a pointer, explain that you will move the piles around and the Mark has to find the ace, but if he finds some other card—like the pointer—he loses (see the line of language above).

Drop the pointer face down back on the pile it came from. Pick up the face-up AS and drop it face down onto the pointer card (that is, back onto its original pile). Now the three packets are reset with a force card on top of each.

THE SNEAKY MOVE: Move the packets around on the table very slowly.

Place your palm-down hands on two packets as if you are palming cards or doing something else suspicious, then lift your hands and place them on two other packets.

You want the Mark to think you are doing some kind of sneaky move.

He expects a sneaky move since you're betting fifty and he's betting five and you wouldn't be doing something that stupid unless you had some kind of advantage.

Greed for the fifty bucks though will outweigh his concerns about his measly five and you can snare him easily as a result.

He points to a pile. You immediately turn the top card of any *other* pile over showing the AS over there. He loses.

THE SECOND BET: Change the bet as explained above and move the piles around again, repeating the suspicious move. Again the Mark loses.

THE THIRD BET: After you turn up the AS, leave it face up and drop it on top of any other pile.

Now turn over the top card of the pile that ace came from to show an odd card as you explain the third bet (that is, if he finds a wrong card, he wins).

Use this card as a pointer during the explanation to subliminally sell the singularity of the ace.

Drop this card, face down, back onto its pile, then pick up the face-up ace and deal it, still face up, to the center of the table.

PREPARING FOR THE KILL: Pick off the top cards of the two piles that still have secret aces on top and drop them face down beside the face-up ace. The Mark thinks these cards are two assorted cards, but they are duplicate aces.

Assemble the deck and place it into the right pocket where the duplicate deck is. The cards won't mix together if you use the card case that's already there as a separator (that is, put the *Svengali* on one side of the case and the duplicate deck on the other).

THE KILL: This leaves the three aces (two face down, one face up) on the table. Turn the face-up ace face down, mix the cards around and have the Mark place his hand on top of a card. Remove the other two cards—don't show their faces—and put them in the right pocket with the rest of the *Svengali* deck. The Mark turns over his card and finds an ace — he loses!

THE CLEAN-UP: Remove the matching ordinary deck and the card case from your pocket. Add the AS and leave the deck on the table for examination.

TWO-CARD MONTE

THE BET: You hold two cards, an ace and a king. You place the cards behind your back and bring one card out face down. The Mark tries to guess which card is still behind your back.

THE OUTCOME: You win or lose as you wish.

THE SCAM: Magic shops sell this trick. It uses two trick cards, a double-faced card and a double-backed card.

For example, the double-faced card might have an ace on one side and a king on the other. The double-backed card is just that: a card with the same back on both sides.

Hold the two cards in the right hand with the double-backed card on top of the double-faced card. Keeping the cards parallel to the floor, spread them slightly to reveal the face of the second card. This looks as if you have a face-down card on top of a face-up card. Name the face-up card; "The king is face-up."

Keeping the cards spread, turn your hand over quickly and as you do so spread the cards the other way by pushing with your thumb and pulling with your fingers. Now the Mark will see the other side of the double-faced card—the ace—and he will assume he sees the back of the king (of course he's just seeing the other side of the double-backed card—the reverse spread you did helps this).

Quickly place the cards behind your back, keeping track of which card is the double-backed card and which face of the double-faced card is where.

Remove the double-backed card and hold it in front of you. Ask the Mark to guess which card is behind your back.

If he guesses the king, bring out the double-faced card showing as an ace. If he names the ace, bring it out showing as the king. To repeat, simply put the cards behind your back and start again. At first, you may wish to bring out the side that makes the Mark a winner. After he wins several times you can take him for double or nothing the last time.

THREE-CARD MONTE

THE BET: Three cards (say an ace, a queen and a deuce) are shown in a fan. The Mark is asked to remember which card is in the middle—it's the queen. The cards are slowly turned face down and the spectator is asked to slowly remove the queen and hold it face down under his hands. His hands completely cover the card.

The remaining two cards are shown (the ace and the deuce). You ask the Mark if he thinks it's possible for you to remove the queen from under his hands without touching him in any way. The Mark says it's impossible and you bet him five bucks you can do it.

THE OUTCOME: As soon as the money is on the table, you tell the Mark to look at the card. When he does he finds it isn't a queen at all, but a message card (usually with the message, "Thanks for the five bucks!").

THE SCAM: This is another little item available in any magic shop. It is sold under several names: "3 Card Monte," "Sucker Card Trick," or "Three Card Monte." There are three cards used: a message card, a flap card and an ordinary card.

The flap card has a small secret flap which does two things: it conceals the message card when the cards are fanned and it masquerades as the card in the middle.

THE SET-UP: You have to set this up in secret. If you are sitting at a table you can take the packet of cards out of your pocket, place them in your lap under the table and set them. You place the message card under the flap, then fan the cards so they look normal.

Now bring the cards forward and make the bet. Turn the cards face down very slowly so that the Mark is absolutely convinced the middle card has not moved.

Have the Mark place his finger on the back of the middle card (really the message card) and slide this card out, still face down, to the table. Have the Mark place both hands on top of the card so that it is completely hidden.

Square the two cards remaining in your hands then turn them over and spread them slightly. The flap will be hidden and the Mark will see what he expects to see: two cards (so the card under his hand must be the original middle card). Now make the bet and collect your cash.

JIGGERY POKERY

THE SCAMARIO

The Hustler and the Mark play a hand of draw poker, standard rules except they both can look through the deck and pick out whatever cards they want and on the draw any player can discard as many cards as he wishes (regular poker rules limit the draw to one, two or three cards, but here a player can discard and draw up to five cards, no draws from the discards). All suits rate equally.

EXPLAINING THE BET TO THE MARK

The Hustler explains that he will go first. The deck will be spread out face up. The Mark will see the Hustler's hand.

The Mark then gets to choose his cards. Then each player can draw.

If the Hustler's hand ties the Mark's, the Mark wins (e.g. two Royal Flushes).

If the Mark's hand beats the Hustler's, the Mark wins.

The Hustler only wins if his hand beats the Mark's, so two out of three times, the Mark will win (the Hustler claims).

THE OUTCOME

The Hustler wins.

THE SECRET

Once the bet has been joined, the Hustler removes the four 10s and any other card to make up his hand.

Marks who are poker players usually respond by taking either the four Aces and a King or a Straight Flush, 9 high; however, it doesn't really matter what they take because they will now shake hands with oblivion on the next move.

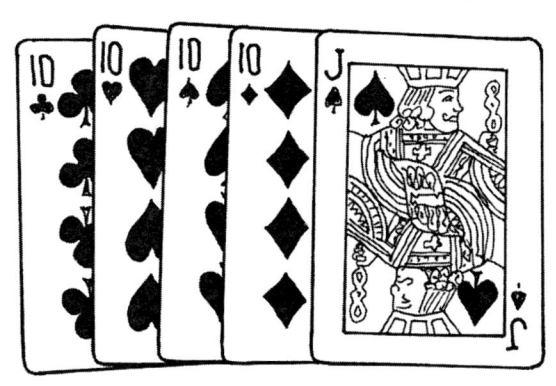

Hustler's initial cards

The Mark's probable choice

THE DRAW

If the Mark has taken four Aces (i.e. Four of a Kind), the Hustler can beat that by discarding the odd card and three of the 10s and making a 10-high Straight Flush (a Straight Flush beats Four of a Kind).

If the Mark took a 9-high Straight Flush, the Hustler can beat that by building a Royal Flush around one of the 10s.

And there is no way the Mark can beat the Hustler's new hand on his draw. First, since the other standard rules of Draw Poker apply, he can't draw from the discards. Second, since the discards include three of the 10s, he can't make either a Royal Flush (to tie and beat the Hustler) or a higher straight.

VERY IMPORTANT

When explaining the bet, make sure that the draw exception is clear: *any or all of the original cards may be discarded and replaced*. In regular Poker, a player is limited to drawing three cards. If the Hustler's hand is a Jack of Diamonds and four 10s, and the three-card draw rule applies, the Mark could draw all Aces and a 9 of Diamonds, thus blocking the Hustler's diamond Straight Flush and winning.

LOADED DICE

> "One of my most precious treasures ... (was) ... an exquisite set of loaded dice, bearing the date of my graduation from high school."
> —W.C. FIELDS

7-11 DICE—LOAD AND FIRE: Real loaded dice are difficult and expensive to come by. But you can "load" ordinary dice in another way—by using ordinary dice in games that you just can't lose, games that you make the rules for, games loaded in your favor.

And magic shops do sell something called *7-11 Dice*. These aren't loaded, they're misspotted, so that one die is all fives and the other all twos and sixes. As a result, these dice can only throw a seven or an eleven (since the only combinations that can come up are 5 + 2 or 5 + 6).

First, I'll describe a game loaded in your favor and then I'll follow that with some brand new scams for *7-11 Dice*, ones never revealed until now.

ANOTHER GAME OF 31

THE GAME: You already know this one—I described it in the marked cards section. The game is somewhat less deceptive with dice, but it works just the same.

You and the Mark alternately turn a die and count to 31 using the values on the top side.

The first person to reach 31 wins. If any one goes over 31, they lose.

THE OUTCOME: You can win or lose, as you like.

THE SCAM: You use a simple system that makes you a winner whenever you want.

PLAY: The Mark turns any side of a die up and calls out its value. For example, he might pick the 6 and say, "Six."

You now get to turn up any other side (that is, you can pick any number as long as it's not the one the Mark just played). He picked a 6 so you can choose the 1, 2, 3, 4 or 5.

You turn up one of the sides, add its value to the Mark's and call out the total.

For example, you might pick the 4, and say, "Ten" (the Mark chose 6, you chose 4—and 6 plus 4 is 10).

Now the Mark responds. He can pick the 6 again, or the ace, 2, 3 or 5, but he can't pick the 4 because you just used it.

Assume he picks the 2; the total is now 12 (6 + 4 + 2 = 12). Now you go again, following the same rule: you can pick any number as long as it isn't the one the Mark just used.

This goes on until a player reaches a total of 31 (this is a win) or a player goes over 31 (this is a loss).

A SAMPLE GAME: **A game might go like this, with you winning:**

Round	Player	Chosen Number	Total
1	Mark	6	6
2	You	4	10
3	Mark	2	12
4	You	5	17
5	Mark	6	23
6	You	1	24
7	Mark	6	30
8	You	1	31

THE DIRTY SECRET: It's the same as with the card version: as long as you make certain magic numbers as the game proceeds you can't lose. As the total changes with each move by the Mark, you always pick a number that will bring you up to the next magic number. The magic numbers are still:

$$3 \quad 10 \quad 17 \quad 24$$

For more details and examples, review "The Game of 31" in the marked cards section.

BONE DRY

The Bet: You and the Mark each throw five bucks into the pot. The Mark begins to shake three dice together in his fist. Asked to pick odd or even, he picks odd. The dice are thrown to the table.

If three odd numbers show up, the Mark wins; if three even numbers show up, you win. If there is a mix of odds and evens, nobody wins and each party throws five more bucks into the pot.

Now it's your turn. You shake the dice and throw them down. If three odd numbers show up, the Mark wins; if three even numbers show up, you win. And, again, if there is a mix of odd and even numbers, nobody wins and each party again throws five bucks into the pot.

This back and forth continues until somebody wins.

THE OUTCOME: You win 100% of the time and leave the Mark bone dry of cash.

THE SCAMS: One of the dice is misspotted—made up entirely of twos and sixes—and you once again make up the rules depending on what the spectator chooses.

7/11 Dice: As I said in the introduction to this chapter, these dice are sold by magic shops. One of the dice is all fives and the other all twos and sixes.

Now you'd think that people would notice something as strange as misspotted dice—but they don't! If you doubt this, have a friend throw the *7-11 Dice* a few times and tell him the dice are loaded with weights. He'll throw them for quite a while before he notices the numbers are all wrong.

In this scam, you only use one of the dice, so detection is even less likely. Of course, if you know a bit of sleight of hand, you can easily switch the trick die out and a fair die in (see *A Simple Dice Switch*, below, for an explanation of such a switch).

Besides the die from the *7-11 Dice* that is all twos and sixes (I'll call that the *2/6 die*), you'll need two ordinary matching dice (same color, same style).

THE TRUE ODDS: Since one of the three dice is made up of only twos and sixes, there are only two possibilities when the dice are thrown:

All even numbers.
A mixture of odd and even numbers.

All odd numbers is impossible; the only winning combination is three even numbers. So, you have to make sure that's the combination the Mark picks for you.

FORCING ODD: The Mark *must* choose all odd as his winning combination. You force him to do this with clever double-talk.

As he shakes the three dice in his fist, you ask:

"What shall we use, odd or even?"

If he replies, "Even," you say:

"Even. Okay, throw the dice down and if three even numbers come up, you lose, but if three odd numbers come up, I win."

If he replies, "Odd," you say:

"Odd. Okay, throw the dice down and if three odd numbers come up, you win the pot, but if three even numbers come up, I win the pot."

You always word it so that you win the pot if three even numbers come up.

What makes this good is the same thing that made "None Out Of Three" (see the Double-Headed coin section) good: of the 8 combinations of three dice, 6 of them are combinations of odd and even numbers *where nobody wins*—and these will occur 75% of the time allowing for a nice fat pot by the time your winner comes up.

And of course there is the fine psychological misdirection of the Mark seeing different combinations of odd and even numbers and thus the use of trick dice seems impossible.

THE FINAL INSULT: Secretly switch out the 2/6 die and switch in the 5 die (see, *A Simple Dice Switch*, below). Now tell the Mark that he can have the all-even bet (it's made money for you and you want to give him a chance): if all even numbers come up, he wins, if all odd come up, you win. With the five die in play you win again.

PAIR OF DICE BY THE DASHBOARD LIGHT

THE GAME: Four dice are used. The Mark takes a pair and you take a pair. Each player throws a dollar in the pot.

You each throw your dice. The higher number wins the pot. If the numbers tie, nobody wins and each player has to add another dollar to the pot. The throws are continued until there is a winner.

THE OUTCOME: You win most of the time.

THE SCAM: One of your dice is the 2/6 die from the *7/11 Dice*. This die tips the odds in your favor so that you will win, according to Professor Lefty Urquhart of the College of Swindling Knowledge, 57% of the time.

A SIMPLE DICE SWITCH

This is very deceptive because instead of switching two dice for two dice, you switch out one of two dice you hold. For example, let's say you've got the 2/6 die hidden in your left hand. To hide it, let your left fingers curl naturally, just as they normally do when the hand is at rest. The die is held by the little finger which curls around it lightly.

The two fair dice are in your right hand. Show the dice on your palm-up right hand. As you turn your right hand over to dump the dice into your left hand, your right little finger curls around one of the dice and holds onto it.

The remaining die falls out of the right hand and into the left hand. The left hand turns and opens to receive it. Of course, as the left hand does this the hidden die is revealed, but the Mark thinks this is one of the dice that just fell into your hand.

To switch out the 2/6 die just reverse the actions: show the dice on your palm-up left hand and curl the little finger around the 2/6 die as the left hand dumps the single die into the right hand.

BET NOIRE

THE GAME: A pair of dice are used. The Mark picks any 4 different numbers out of the numbers 1 to 6. For example, the Mark decides on 2, 3, 4, 5. The Hustler gets the remaining two numbers (in this example, 1 and 6).

The dice are thrown: if either die has one of the Hustler's numbers, the Hustler wins, otherwise, the Hustler loses. For example, the throw is 1, 4: the Hustler wins. If the throw had been 2,3, the Hustler loses.

Since the Mark has twice as many chances as winning as the Hustler, money is bet 2 to 1. The Mark lays down $2, the Hustler lays down $1.

THE OUTCOME: The Hustler wins 52% of the time, but since the betting is at 2 to 1—the Mark risks $2 for every $1 the Hustler risks—the Hustler risks less when he loses and makes more when he wins.

THE SCAM: Here the odds are misstated. It sounds perfectly reasonable to say that the Mark has twice as many chances to win as the Hustler since the Mark has four numbers and the Hustler has only 2 (and this provides the rationale for the 2 to 1 betting). However, if you examine the chart below, and assuming the Hustler's numbers are 1 and 6 (i.e., if any pair contains a 1 *or* a 6, the Hustler wins), you'll see that there are 19 winning combinations for the Hustler (19/36 = 52%).

This works for any two different numbers the Hustler ends up with. Say the numbers are 2, 3. This combination also provides 19 winners.

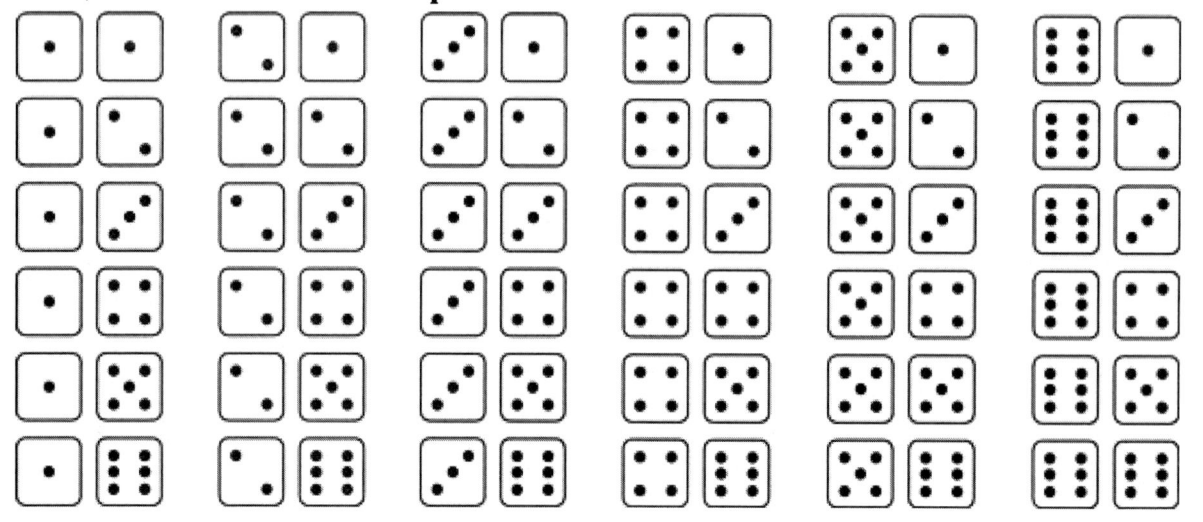

MONTE BONES

(Illustrations by Tony Dunn)

"Monte Bones" is something brand new in scambling, something that I'm sure will keep you busy experimenting for months.

It has all the features of "Three Card Monte" and "The Shell Game," but it's much easier to learn, has no angles, can be performed on any surface and everything can be examined before and after (plus, if using the impromptu version, you can eat the evidence).

THE GAME

You show three cubes two blanks and one cube with a single red spot and allow the Mark to examine them.

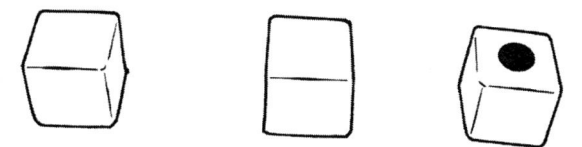

You turn the spotted cube spot side down—

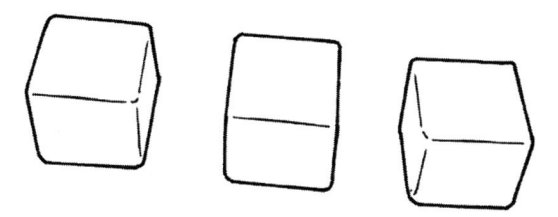

—and mix the three cubes around on the table.

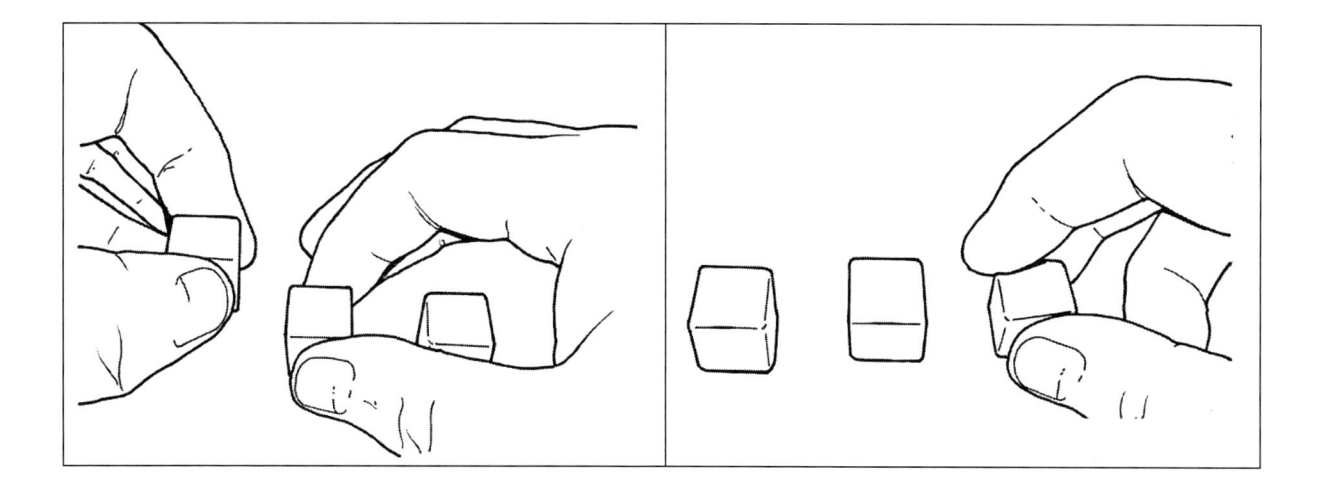

THE OUTCOME

The Mark can never find the spotted cube.

THE CUBES

The basic set of cubes consists of two blanks and a spotted cube.

You can easily make these yourself: buy some cheap poker dice, sand the faces of three of the dice clean and put a red dot on one of them. Alternately, sand all of the faces clean with the exception of the Ace of Spades face and use that face in place of the red dot.

THE SECRET

After the cubes are moved around on the table, the selected cube is picked up and its underside apparently shown. In fact, a secret move, the Double Turnover, is used to show one of the blank sides, the real underside being hidden by the thumb.

To see how this works, hold the spot cube between thumb and forefinger with the spot up (note in the routine the spot will be *down*, but for the purposes of this explanation, it is up for clarity).

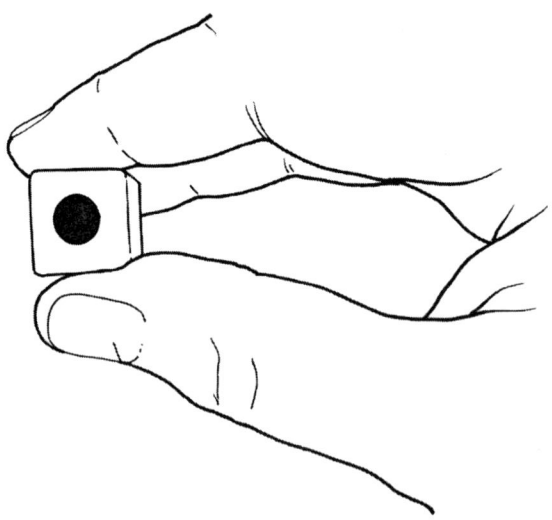

Turn the right hand palm up to show the underside of the cube.

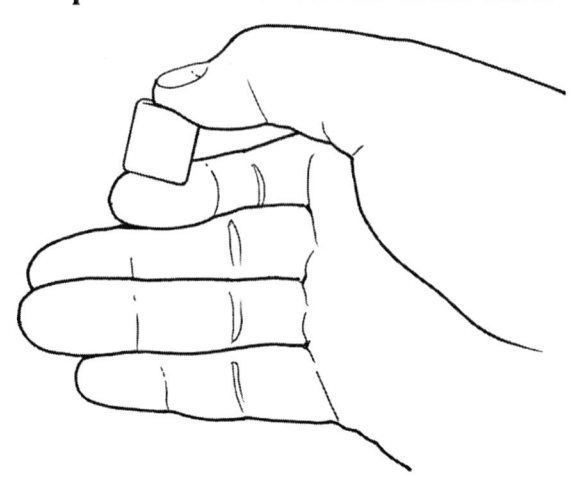

However, as you do that, your right thumb pushes on the cube, rotating it a quarter turn.

As the hand is turned palm down, the secret rotation is made in the opposite direction (but still in the same direction as the motion of the hand turning) so that you end up in the starting position.

These are small motions, not wide arm swings.

Remember, the secret rotation is made in the same direction as the motion of the hand (i.e., clockwise as the hand turns palm up clockwise, and counterclockwise as the hand is turned palm down counterclockwise).

Learn to do the Double Turnover with either hand—it makes the routine easier because you can use your left hand for the cube on the left and your right for the cube on the right or in the middle).

Detailed descriptions of this move can be found in "Sack's Spotted Sorcery" (*Phoenix* #152, p. 615) and in Bruce Elliott's *Classic Secrets of Magic* (p. 36).

THE MODIFIED MOVE

The Double-Turnover Move needs a bit of help when you do it after picking a cube off the table because the cube is not in the correct position after the pickup.

Try this: place the spotted cube, spot side down, on the table.

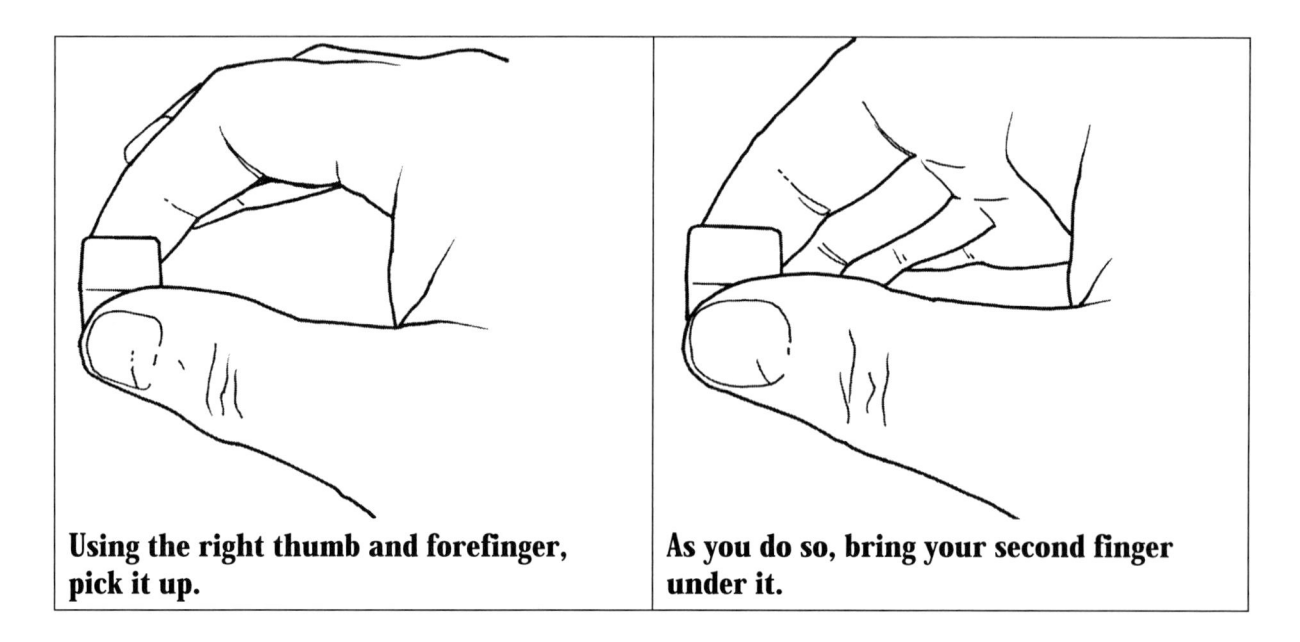

Using the right thumb and forefinger, pick it up.	As you do so, bring your second finger under it.

SIDE VIEWS

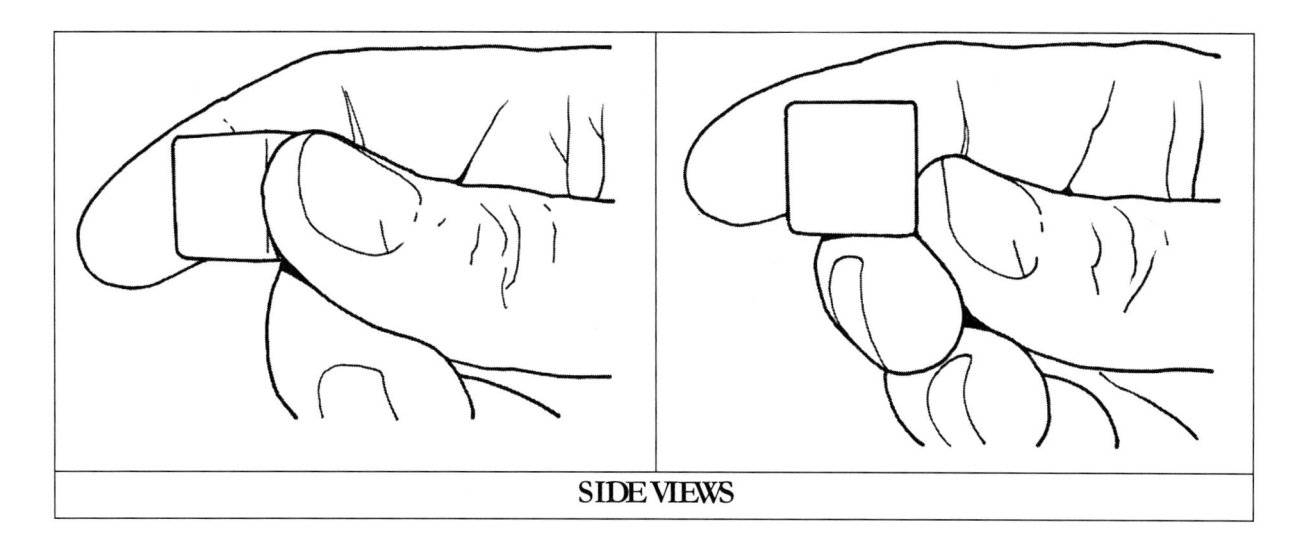

Slide your right thumb further down the side of the cube until it touches the second finger.

This positions your thumb in the best position for the secret rotation.

Move your second finger away and turn your hand over doing the Double Turnover as you do.

Show the apparent underside of the cube

it's blank, the red spot is hidden by your thumb. Turn your hand palm down, doing the Double Turnover in reverse, and place the cube back on the table.

The red spot is now touching the table.

THE ROUTINE

Here's a general routining idea. Place the cubes in a row, with a blank on the left, a blank in the middle and the red spot—spot side up—on the right.

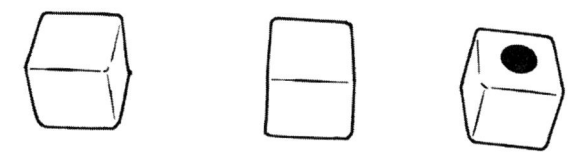

Turn the spotted cube, red spot down.

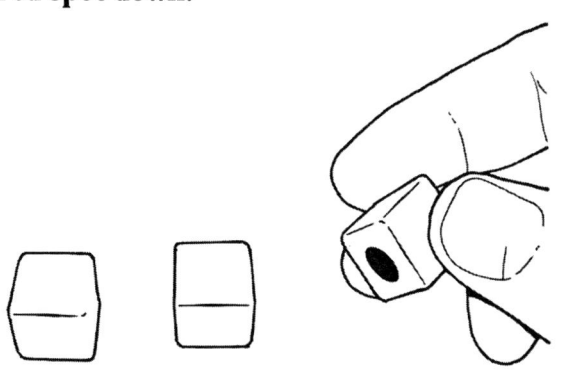

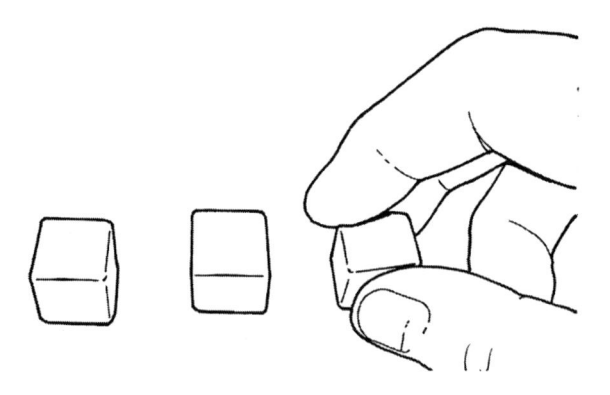

Pick up the left cube in the left hand and the right cube (the spotted cube in the right).

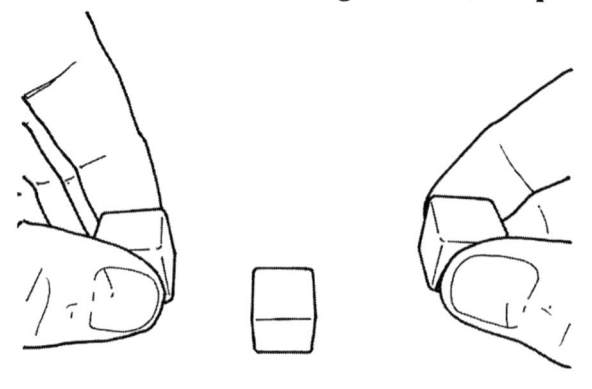

Place the right hand's cube on the left, as the left hand moves up and out of the way.

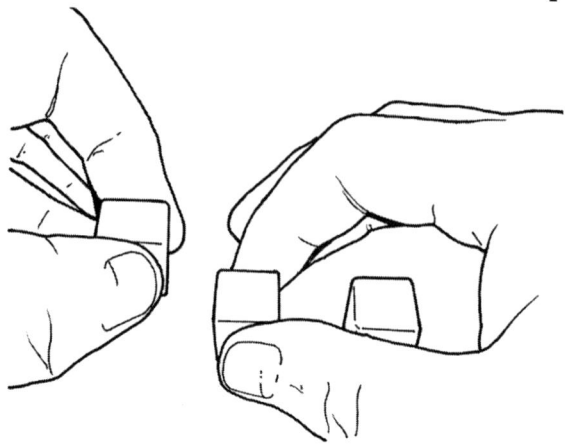

As the empty right hand moves to the right, it grabs the middle cube.

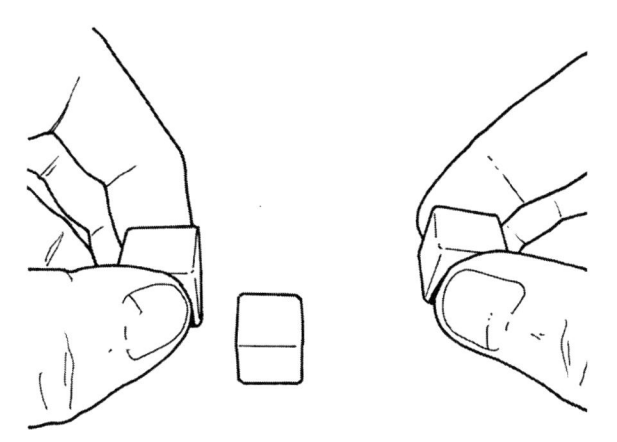

The left hand places its cube on the right.

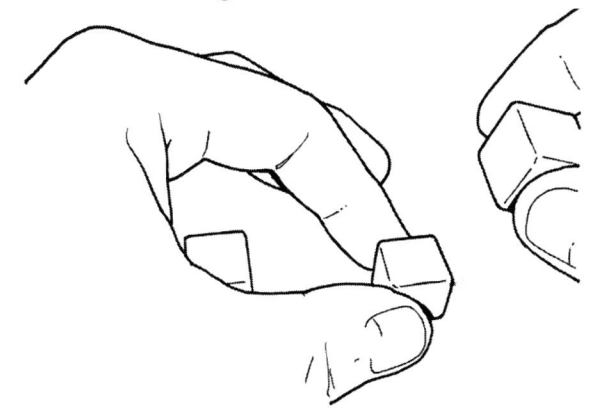

The right hand moves left and places its cube in the middle. The spotted cube is now on the left.

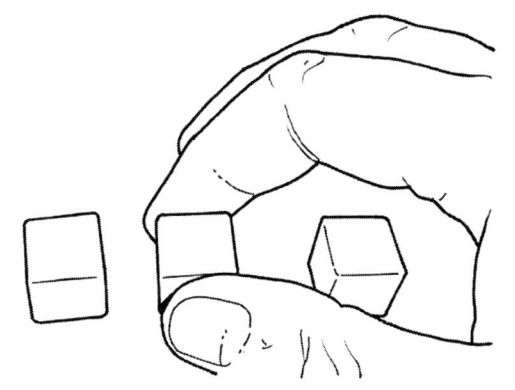

Push the cubes together.

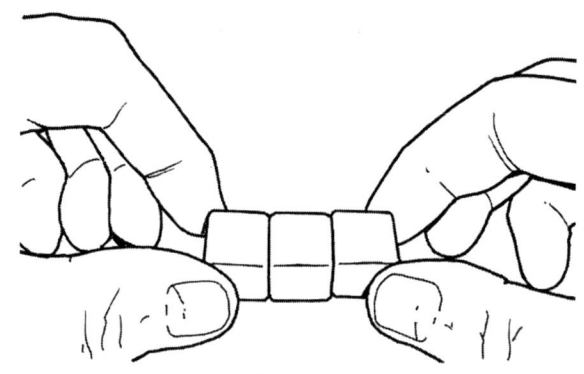

Pick up the two cubes on the right and jump them to the left over the remaining cube.

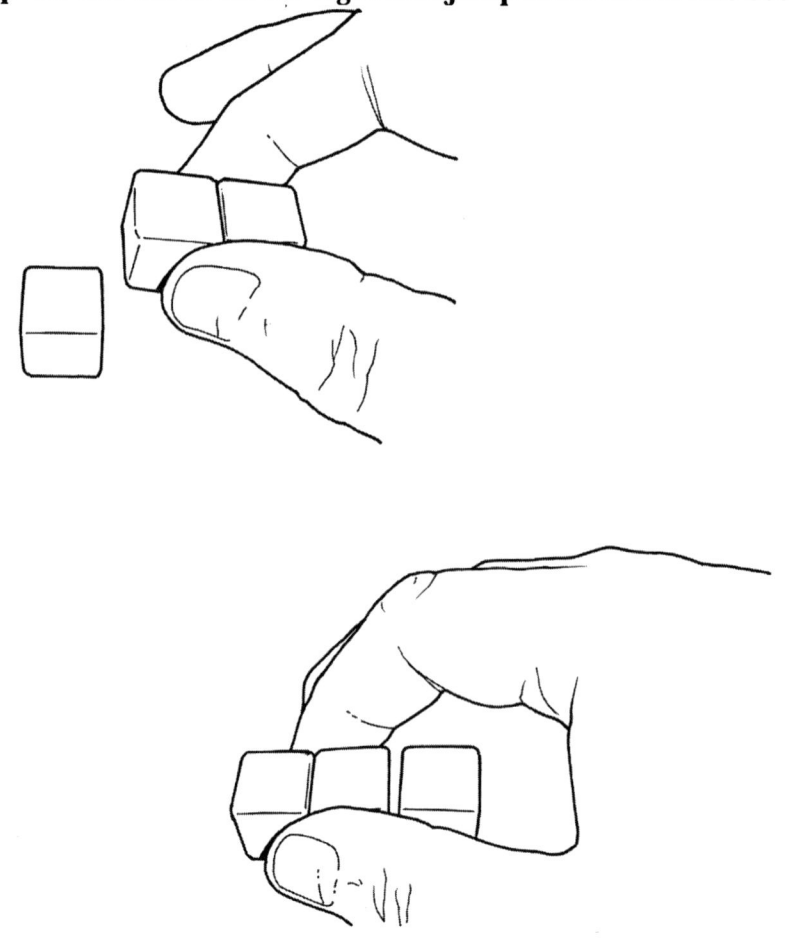

Repeat this move twice, then move the cubes apart (the spotted cube will be on the left).

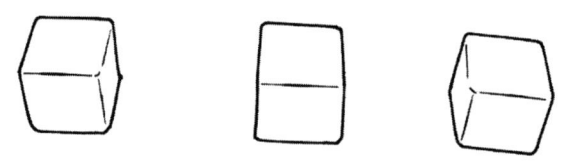

Ask the spectator to point to the red cube. If he gets it right, use the Double Turnover to show him he's wrong.

If he gets it wrong, pick up the cube and show him he's wrong.

OTHER IDEAS

Using a set of three cubes with two red dots (i.e. one blank and two spotted cubes) you can use the Double Turnover to apparently display two blanks and a red spot. This setup has the advantage that not only can you show the spectator has lost every time, but every time you can show the red spot was somewhere else.

To finesse this idea, have the two spotted cubes heavily loaded so that when all three cubes are rolled out, one red spot is always up and one is always down and hidden—this would be very disarming.

I had a custom set of cubes made up with a large and somewhat depressed spots. This way I can feel which cubes have the spots with my fingers and don't have to look.

You can use sugar cubes for an impromptu version simply add a black dot to one cube with a pen. If secretly using more than one dot, you can always eat the evidence if called.

Using dice switches, you can switch in cubes with green and black spots. For a magical ending, these spots appear.

You don't need to start with three cubes—a more interesting routine might be possible with four cubes on the table.

GAME OF BONES
(Illustrations by Tony Dunn)

It turns out the late Peter Kane and I were thinking along similar lines but independently and in different countries.

Peter's idea appeared as "Di-A-Monte" in Harry Lorayne's *Apocalypse*, Vol. 17, #7, July, 1994). With Harry's permission, I am describing the Kane routine, but using my method and some routining changes, so it's about 50% Kane, 50% Farmer.

Peter used the same dot-on-a-blank-cube idea, and the same Double Turnover to hide the spot at the appropriate times, but when he tabled the cube the secret spot would be facing him, not facing down. So, he had to perform with the spectators directly in front of him.

I prefer my approach because the routine can be performed surrounded. The small adjustment required to do the Double Turnover (the second finger pushing the cube up slightly) is never noticed.

For the Kane/Farmer routine, you'll need three white cubes, two of which have red spots and a fourth red cube which has a white spot.

Place the white cubes in one pocket and the red cube in another.

1. Remove the three white cubes without flashing the spots and arrange them on the table from left to right with the spots facing down and hidden, spot cubes in the middle and on the right.

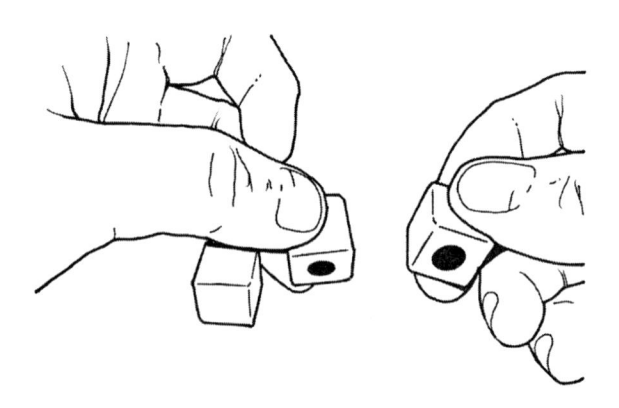

2. Pick up the leftmost cube and show its bottom as blank then replace it. Pick up the center cube and use the Double Turnover to show its bottom as blank, replace it. Pick up the cube on the right, and show the spot on the bottom, then replace it, spot down. You are back to the starting position.

3. Move the three cubes around in the usual confusing fashion and ask the Mark to guess where the red spot is. He picks a cube and you show it does not have a spot. Do this twice.

You don't need to actually know where the spotted cubes are, simply use the Turnover Move every time to always show a blank bottom on the cube picked.

Pick up one of the remaining cubes and show its bottom—if it doesn't have a spot, pick up the remaining cube and show its underside because it will have a spot.

4. Repeat the "game."

5. At the end of the second, "game:" you've just shown one of the cubes with a spot, so one of the two others must be the other spotted cube.

Pick them both up and steal a secret glance at their undersides as you gesture—pocket the cube *without* the secret spot and tell the spectator you are going to make it even easier for him.

6. Bring out the red cube from your pocket being careful not to flash its white spot.

Explain that the odds have changed from 2 to 1 against him to even money because he *knows* the white cube is blank and that one of the white cubes is spotted.

7. Show the spot on the white cube, then place it spot side down on the table and move the three cubes around in a confusing manner.

There are now two white cubes on the table, both with spots, and the red cube with a secret spot.

Have the spectator pick a white cube. Pick it up and using the Double Turnover show it is blank. Pick up the other white cube and show the spot on the bottom.

8. Tell the spectator you'll make it even easier for him, a sure thing—pocket the white cube you've just shown as a no-spot cube. Just the white and red cubes remain.

Show the spot on the bottom of the white cube and, using the Double Turnover, show the bottom of the red cube as blank.

Replace the cubes on the table, spot sides down.

9. Move the two cubes around and ask the spectator to pick, "the cube with the *spot*."

Naturally, he picks the white cube. Show it as blank and then show the spot on the bottom of the red cube to end.

OIL & WATER DICE

THE PROPS
You need three white dice and three black dice.

THE BET
The Hustler arranges the dice as shown. The dice alternate in color. The numbers on top are used here for the purposes of explanation; in practice, the numbers can be random.

The Hustler makes three moves. Each move uses two adjacent dice. He ends as shown: the dice separated, white on the left, black on the right.

The Hustler arranges the dice in the starting position and challenges the Mark to duplicate what he just did.

THE MOVES
There is no scam here; the secret is simply to know how to make the moves. Start here:

Move the 2-3 to the left end of the row.

Move the 5-6 into the space left by the 2/3.

Move the 6-4 to the left end of the row.

SCAM

To make this a scam, do the sequence once and point out the white dice are on the *left* and the black dice are on the *right*. When you set up the dice a second time, rather than alternating them black/white, from left to right, alternate them white/black from left to right. This way, even if the Mark nails the sequence of moves, he'll end up with the black dice on the left end, and the white dice on the right end, the opposite of the objective.

5-3-4-1-6-2

The Hustler lines up the dice from left to right, so the numbers read 5-3-4-1-6-2, because this is the number he plays the lottery with.

The Hustler makes three moves. Each move uses two adjacent dice. He ends as shown: the dice in 1-2-3-4-5-6 order.

No matter how the Mark tries, he cannot duplicate the feat.

THE SCAM

A secret move is made as the dice are rearranged. Without the secret move, the final arrangement is impossible to achieve. The move is the Double Turnover, described above in the "Monte Bones" routine.

THE MOVES

Line the dice up as shown: however, set the 1, so that the side facing you is showing a 2 and set the 2, so the side facing you is showing a 1.

Move the 3-4 to the left end of the row.

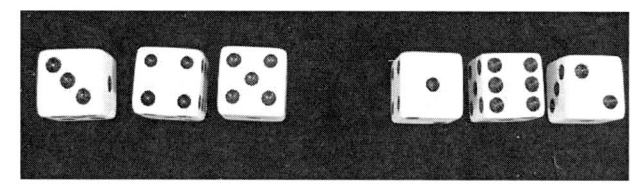

Move the 6-2 to the space left by the 3-4.

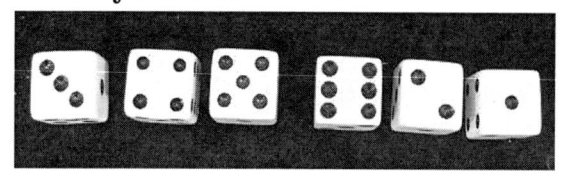

Pick up the 2-1 pair from the right end of the row.

As your right hand moves left, use the Double Turnover to revolve the dice a quarter turn forward.

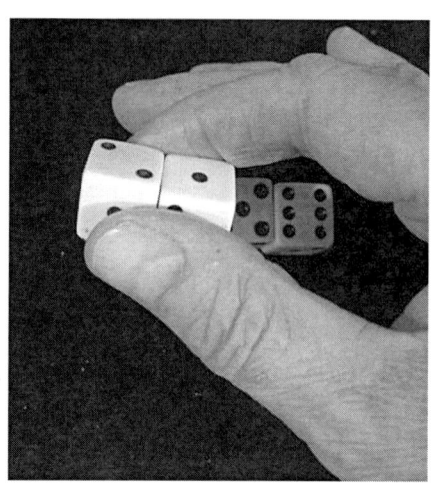

As the secret move ends, the 2-1 combination has been secretly switched for a 1-2 combination and the dice are placed at the left end of the row to create the 1-2-3-4-5-6 sequence.

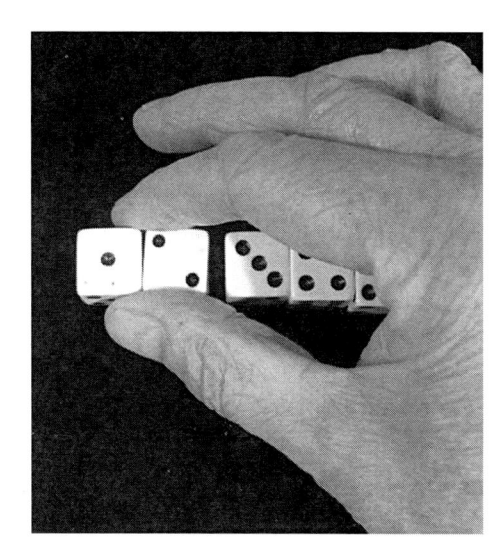

Challenge the Mark to duplicate your feat. Of course, he won't be able to.

To add another layer of confusion for the Mark, rather than use 6 white dice, use three black and three white and alternate the colors as in "Oil and Water Dice," above. At the end the colors are separated and the dice are in 1-2-3-4-5-6 order. The color separation happens automatically as a byproduct of the moves.

ALTERNATE HANDLING

If you have trouble picking up two dice with one hand and doing the secret move, use two hands: the left thumb and forefinger taking the left die and the right thumb and forefinger taking the right die. As you move left, do the secret move with each hand at the same time.

It's even possible to do no move at all: with two hands on the dice, and as you move left, revolve your hands inward so your thumbs are on top and table the dice.

BACKGROUND

These scams are my very different versions of a dice scam described by Bill Miesel, Ed Eckl and Harry Hirschvogel in *Precursor* LXIX.

COUNT DICEULA

THE GAME

You and the Mark each hold a die and take turns adding the sides. The first person to reach 50 wins. For example, the Mark goes first and shows a 5. You show a 3 to make a total of 8. The Mark shows a 6 to make a new total of 14. This continues to 50 and you win.

THE SCAM

The numbers you choose are selected so that you capture the following key numbers for yourself

8, 15, 22, 29, 36, 43.

For example, the Mark shows a 2 so you show a 6 to make a total of 8, your first key number. After you reach 8, always select a number that together with your Mark's number equals 7.

A sample game might run s shown in the drawing.

Always make your choice of a number seem random. Shake the die in your hands. Mull over your decision.

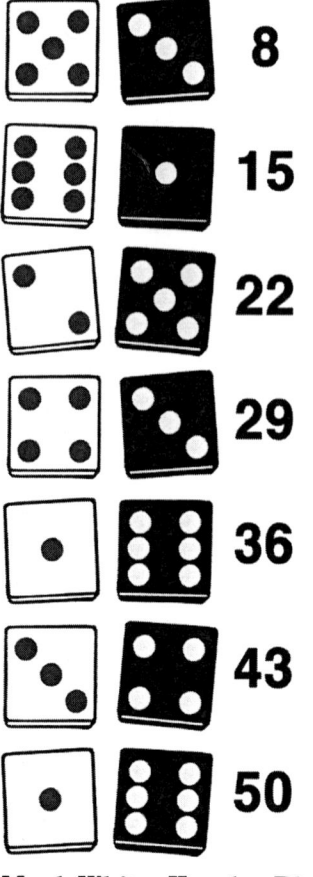

    5 3   8
    6 1 15
    2 5 22
    4 3 29
    1 6 36
    3 4 43
    1 6 50

Mark White, Hustler Black

THE CHICAGO BAR SCAM

> "The chances are you'll get off with life.
> That means if you're a good girl,
> you'll be out in twenty years.
> I'll be waiting for you."
> —Humphrey Bogart, The Maltese Falcon

You're sitting at the end of the bar and you have determined that the time is right to move into your pitch.

You ask the bartender to write his name on one of his twenty dollar bills. He does so and then folds it into eighths.

THE BET

You bet twenty bucks against the bartender's twenty bucks that you can make the bartender's signed bill vanish and appear in the cash register at the other end of the bar.

As this is obviously impossible, and you are obviously insane, the bartender immediately takes your bet. Of course, the small crowd of barflies surrounding you may even offer some side bets, all of which you offer to cover.

THE SCAMARIO

You pick up the bill and place it up under a bar napkin, which drapes over and around the bill. Your other hand pinches the bill through the material.

You ask the bartender to reach up under the napkin and confirm the bill is still there. He does so. You turn to the barflies and they all reach up under and check that the bill is still there.

Turn back to the bartender and say the magic phrase, "Perscripto in manibus tabellariorum est," (The check is in the mail). The napkin flutters open

The twenty is gone.

The bartender walks down to the other end of the bar, opens the cash register and finds his signed bill. You collect it (and your side bets), saddle up and ride out.

PAY NO ATTENTION TO THE MAN BEHIND THE CURTAIN

The man (or woman) in this case is your covert confederate playing the part of one of the barflies. The confederate is the last person to check under the napkin for the bill and he steals it.

With the bill secretly in hand, this barfly fades into the background as you stall for time. The barfly goes to the other end of the bar and orders a $3 drink, paying for it with the signed bill (which by this time has been unfolded). Pocketing the $17 in change, the barfly quaffs the drink and heads for the door.

You open the napkin to reveal the vanish and the bartender discovers the signed bill in the far cash register. You collect $20 (plus the side bets) and leave. When added to the $17 your friend got in change, you've just scammed $37 and a free drink. Using a twenty makes it unlikely that the signed bill will be handed out in change before you get a chance to slam the scam home.

UPDATE

David Blaine liked this so much he explained it in Esquire magazine. His version didn't use a bar napkin—he simply palmed the bill and passed it off to a passing confederate (this is much harder to get away with!).

The magazine included a warning

> "Esquire's legal counsel ... (notes) ... that ... (this) ... confidence trick is highly illegal and should not be attempted. In fact, the only reason we're explaining it here, in print, is to alert America's bartenders ... to this nefarious con so that they may better protect themselves from unscrupulous patrons."

I second that.

Recently, I found evidence that this must be a very old scam indeed. "The Vanishing Pound Note" is explained at page 122 of Derek Lever's book, *Ken Brooke and Friends Volume One* (Taurus Magic Supply 1986).

In Ken's version (which has to go back to the 1950s), he borrows the bill from the bartender and has it signed.

The signed bill is covered with a handkerchief and secretly palmed away. After showing that the bill has vanished, Ken takes out a cigarette, hands it to the bartender and tells him the bill is inside.

The bartender discovers it isn't—Ken shrugs his shoulders and carries on with other tricks. Meanwhile, he has passed the bill off to a confederate who buys a drink at the other end of the bar.

Eventually, the bartender demands his bill back, and Ken tells him to look in the cash register at the other end of the bar.

CHICAGO BAR CARD SCAM

THE BET

The Mark is given a deck of cards, told to shuffle it and cut to any card (it can be his deck and it doesn't have to be complete).

He shows the card to everyone except you, then reassembles the deck and shuffles it. He secretly writes the name of the card on a twenty dollar bill and folds the bill so you can't see the writing.

You lay forty bucks on top of his twenty and make the following bet:

> "I'm willing to bet my forty against your twenty that I can make a series of statements about your card and every single one will be right.
>
> "If I make a mistake, I get one and only one chance to actually name your card.
>
> "If I can't name your card, the money's all yours.

"So, I might say your card is red. If I'm wrong, because it's black, I have to name it right then or you win.

"You have to play fair with me and simply tell me if my statements are right or wrong.

"And I will never ask you the name of your card before I tell you what it is. If I do—I lose."

THE SCAM

This sounds completely impossible, but you can't lose. Assume the Mark has written, "Ace of Spades" on his twenty. Of course, you don't know this. The real purpose of the writing is simply to ensure that he doesn't scam you by changing his mind.

Pick up the deck and deal the top card face up (assume the Queen of Hearts). Say:

"Okay, I bet that this is not your card."

There are only two possibilities, either this is his card or it isn't and he has to tell you whether you're right or wrong.

If it isn't, you have made a true statement since you've said it isn't his card.

If it is his card, you're wrong (remember he has to tell you whether you're right or wrong). You have made a mistake, but you can now name his card.

So, you simply deal through the deck making the same bet on every card until you're wrong, then you name the card and collect the money.

Beat'em, Cheat'em, Leave'em Bleedin' Another Bammo Magic Public Service

-30-